How Does Sound Change?

Robin Johnson

Crabtree Publishing Company
www.crabtreebooks.com

Author
Robin Johnson

Publishing plan research and development
Reagan Miller

Editorial director
Kathy Middleton

Editor
Kathy Middleton

Proofreader
Shannon Welbourn

Design
Samara Parent

Photo research
Samara Parent

**Production coordinator
and prepress technician**
Samara Parent

Print coordinator
Margaret Amy Salter

Illustrations
Jeanette McNaughton-Julich: page 19

Photographs
Thinkstock: title page, pages 12, 14
Simon Speed/wikipedia: page 13
All other images by Shutterstock

Library and Archives Canada Cataloguing in Publication

Johnson, Robin (Robin R.), author
    How does sound change? / Robin Johnson.

(Light and sound waves close-up)
Includes index.
Issued in print and electronic formats.
ISBN 978-0-7787-0520-8 (bound).--ISBN 978-0-7787-0524-6 (pbk.).--
ISBN 978-1-4271-9009-3 (html).--ISBN 978-1-4271-9013-0 (pdf)

    1. Sound--Juvenile literature. 2. Sound-waves--Juvenile
literature. I. Title.

QC225.5.J64 2014   j534   C2014-900805-8
                                        C2014-900806-6

Library of Congress Cataloging-in-Publication Data

CIP available at Library of Congress

Crabtree Publishing Company

www.crabtreebooks.com   1-800-387-7650

Printed in the USA/052014/SN20140313

**Published in Canada
Crabtree Publishing**
616 Welland Ave.
St. Catharines, Ontario
L2M 5V6

**Published in the United States
Crabtree Publishing**
PMB 59051
350 Fifth Avenue, 59th Floor
New York, New York 10118

**Published in the United Kingdom
Crabtree Publishing**
Maritime House
Basin Road North, Hove
BN41 1WR

**Published in Australia
Crabtree Publishing**
3 Charles Street
Coburg North
VIC 3058

Contents

What is sound?

Sound is all the noises you hear each day. People, animals, and objects make sounds. Your cat meows to tell you it is hungry. Your alarm clock buzzes to get you out of bed. Your classroom can get very noisy with the activities of so many children in one room!

Your teacher reads books to you out loud at story time.

Sounds all around

There are different sounds in different places. You can hear car horns honking on busy city streets or cows mooing in country meadows. In back yards, there are birds chirping and children playing noisy games. Name some other sounds that you hear people, animals, and objects make.

Good vibrations

All sounds are made by **vibrations**.

A vibration is a quick motion back and forth.

You can see a vibration by stretching elastic

bands between your fingers and

having a friend pluck them

with their finger. The

elastics will **vibrate**.

To vibrate is to make

a vibration.

Small vibrations

Everything makes vibrations, but you cannot always see them. Sometimes the motion is too small for us to see. Even a feather will make a small vibration when it hits the ground. However, the movement back and forth is so small you can't see the vibration or hear the sound.

Sound waves

The vibration of an object makes **sound waves**. A sound wave carries the vibration from place to place. The wave travels from the object that is vibrating to your ear. Ears catch sound waves and carry them to your brain. Your brain tells you what sounds you are hearing.

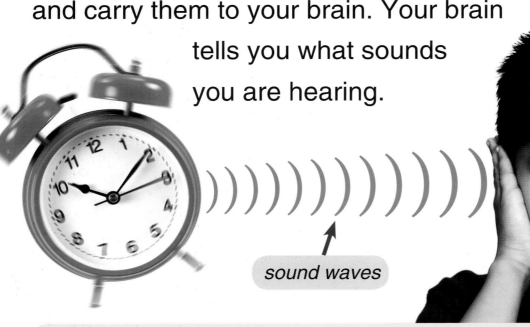

sound waves

The vibrations from the alarm clock are carried by sound waves to this boy's ear. His brain is telling him, "It's time to go!"

Spreading out

A sound wave starts when an object vibrates. Then the wave spreads out from the object in all directions, just like ripples do when you drop something in the water. If you are close enough to the sound wave, you will hear it with your ears.

Turn it down!

Different sounds have different **volumes**. Volume is how loud or soft a sound is. Some sounds are so loud that they hurt your ears! You put your hands over your ears to keep out the noise. Other sounds are so soft that you can hardly hear them at all.

The power of sound

Sound is a form of **energy**. Sounds have different volumes because some sound waves have more energy than others. A strong sound wave has a lot of energy. It makes a loud noise that you can hear from far away. A weaker sound wave has less energy and makes less noise.

What do you think?

Name some sounds that are loud and some sounds that are soft. Why are they different volumes?

Pitch perfect

Different sounds also have different **pitches**. Pitch is how high or low a sound is. Whistles, sirens, and screams are high sounds. Rolling thunder, hooting owls, and horns on big ships are all low sounds.

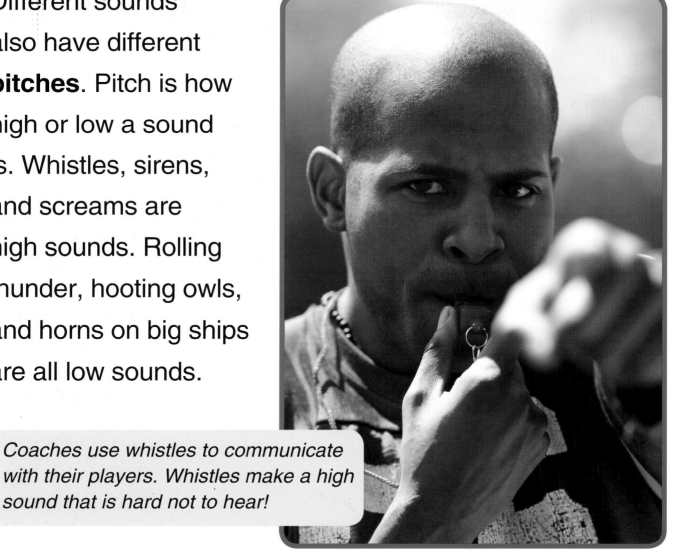

Coaches use whistles to communicate with their players. Whistles make a high sound that is hard not to hear!

Pitch changes

Pitch changes when the motion of vibrations in sound waves speed up or slow down. When vibrations move back and forth very fast, sounds have a high pitch. When vibrations move more slowly, sounds have a low pitch.

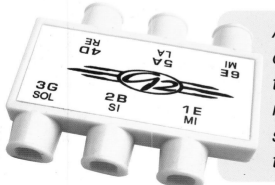

A singer will blow on a pitch pipe to make sure the note he or she is singing reaches the right pitch.

*Musical instruments make **notes**. A note is a musical sound with a certain pitch. When you strum a thin, light string on a guitar, it vibrates quickly and makes a high note. When you strum a thick, heavy string, it vibrates slowly and makes a low note.*

Sound travels

Sound waves travel through air and water. They also travel through solid materials such as wood and steel. If sound did not travel through walls and other solid objects, you might not hear your mother calling you for dinner!

Sound travels through the air on waves, much like this Frisbee.

Silent space

Sound waves cannot travel in space. There are wide areas between planets and stars that are empty. There is not even any air. Sound waves need something to travel through, such as air. Because sound waves cannot travel in space, there is no sound in space.

What do you think?

What would happen if you sneezed in space? Would it make a sound? Or would it just make a mess?

Waves in water

How quickly a sound wave moves depends on what it is traveling through. A sound wave moves faster through water than it does through air. It moves even faster through solid objects, such as walls.

It is hard to hear clearly under water. When water fills our ears, our **eardrums** cannot vibrate to send sound signals to the brain.

Whales sing different songs to communicate different kinds of information to other whales.

Water world

Some animals that live in water use sounds to **communicate** with one another. To communicate is to share information. Whales live in oceans. Some whales communicate by making noises that sound like songs. Other whales can hear the songs even when they are very far away—even as far as a hundred miles (160 km)!

Sound bounces

Some sound waves bounce off objects and return to the place where the sound began. Sound waves that bounce back are called **echoes**. You can make an echo by standing far away from a big wall or steep mountain. Shout and your words will come back to you!

Animal echoes

Some animals use echoes to help them move around in the dark. Bats make clicking sounds with their tongues. The sounds bounce off of trees and other objects in their path. The echoes come back to the bats and help guide them safely around the objects.

What do you think?

Dolphins make whistling sounds that come back to them as echoes. How do you think echoes help dolphins swim and hunt in the deep, dark ocean?

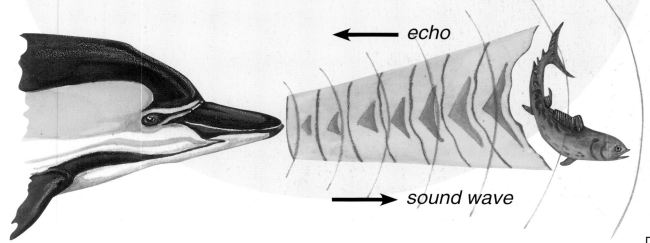

echo

sound wave

Pipe up!

Follow these steps to make a panpipe. A panpipe is a musical instrument made up of tubes. Each tube is a different length and makes a different note when you blow air into it.

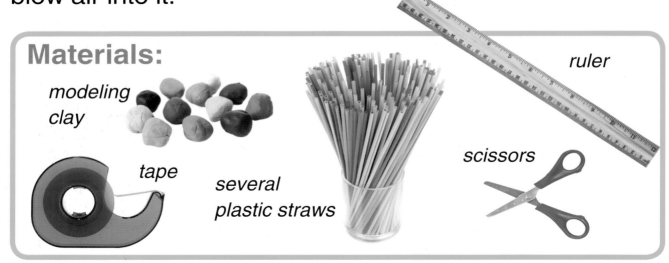

Materials:

modeling clay

tape

several plastic straws

scissors

ruler

What to do:

1. Cut the straws into different lengths. Each straw should be about a half inch (1 cm) shorter than the one beside it.

2. Line up the straws in a row from longest to shortest. Tape the straws together.

3. Roll some clay into small balls. Push one ball of clay into the bottom of each straw at the uneven end.

4. Hold the pipes straight up and down in front of you with the open ends of the straws facing up. Blow gently across the open ends. Make sure you don't cover the ends completely with your lips.

5. Play your panpipe and make some music!

Making waves

Your panpipe shows you that different vibrations make different sounds. Sound waves move in and out of the short straws quickly. These fast vibrations make high notes. It takes more time for sound waves to travel through the long straws. Slower vibrations make lower notes.

What do you think?

What happens if you blow hard on the panpipe? Do the sounds get louder or softer? Why does the volume change?

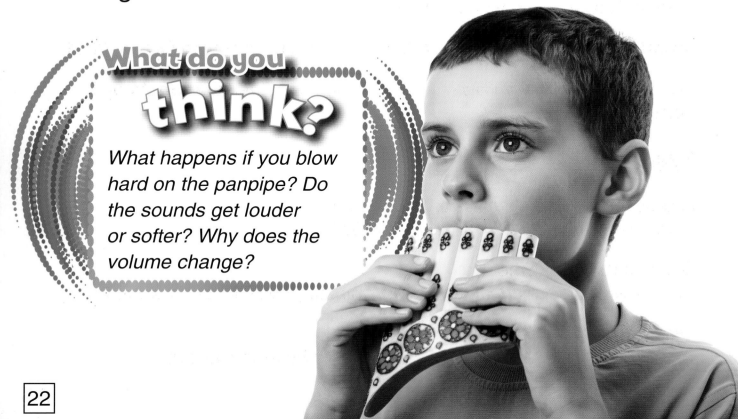

Learning More

Books

What Are Sound Waves? by Robin Johnson. Crabtree, 2014.

Different Sounds by Charlotte Guillain. Heinemann, 2009.

Exploring Sound by Claire Llewellyn. Sea to Sea Publications, 2008.

Hands-On Science: Sound and Light by Jack Challoner and Maggie Hewson. Kingfisher, 2013.

Investigating Sound by Sally M. Walker. Lerner Publishing Group, 2011.

Loud or Soft? High or Low?: A Look at Sound by Jennifer Boothroyd. Lerner Classroom, 2011.

Websites

Science Kids: The Science of Sound for Kids
http://www.sciencekids.co.nz/sound.html

Science Kids at Home
http://www.sciencekidsathome.com/science_topics/what_is_sound.html

Dialogue for Kids: What Is Sound?
http://idahoptv.org/dialogue4kids/season14/sound/facts.cfm

Words to know

communicate (kuh-MYOO-ni-keyt) *verb* To share ideas and information

eardrum (EER-druhm) *noun* Part of the ear that vibrates and moves tiny bones inside the ear

echo (EK-oh) *noun* A sound wave that bounces back and is heard again

energy (EN-er-jee) *noun* The power to do work

note (noht) *noun* A musical sound with a certain pitch

pitch (pich) *noun* How high or low a sound is

sound wave (sound weyv) *noun* Something that carries the vibration of sound

vibrate (VAHY-breyt) *verb* To move quickly back and forth

vibration (vahy-BREY-shuh n) *noun* A fast movement back and forth

volume (VOL-yoom) *noun* How loud or soft a sound is

A noun is a person, place, or thing. A verb is an action word that tells you what someone or something does.

Index